# DUINO ELEGIES

# RAINER MARIA RILKE

In Translations by M. D. HERTER NORTON
*Letters to a Young Poet*
*Sonnets to Orpheus*
*Wartime Letters to Rainer Maria Rilke*
*Translations from the Poetry of Rainer Maria Rilke*
*The Lay of the Love and Death of Cornet Christopher Rilke*
*The Notebooks of Malte Laurids Brigge*
*Stories of God*

Translated by JANE BANNARD GREENE and M. D. HERTER NORTON
*Letters of Rainer Maria Rilke*
Volume One, 1892–1910     Volume Two, 1910–1926

Translated by DAVID YOUNG
*Duino Elegies*

In Various Translations
*Rilke on Love and Other Difficulties*
Translations and Considerations of Rainer Maria Rilke
Compiled by JOHN J. L. MOOD

*Rainer Maria Rilke*

# DUINO ELEGIES

*A New Translation, with an
Introduction and Commentary, by*

*David Young*

W · W · NORTON & COMPANY

New York · London

This translation was originally published in FIELD,
*Contemporary Poetry and Poetics*, issues 5 through 9

Copyright 1978 by W. W. Norton & Company, Inc.
All Rights Reserved

Reissued in a Norton paperback edition 1992

Library of Congress Cataloging in Publication Data

Rilke, Rainer Maria, 1875–1926.
Duino Elegies.

Translation of Duineser Elegien.
I. Young, David P. II. Title.
PT2635.165D82    1978    831'.9'12    78–2816

ISBN 0-393-30931-2

W. W. Norton & Company, Inc.
500 Fifth Avenue, New York, N. Y. 10110
W. W. Norton & Company Ltd
10 Coptic Street, London WC1A 1PU

PRINTED IN THE UNITED STATES OF AMERICA

6    7    8    9    0

# Contents

# Introduction

We have a marvelous, almost legendary, image of the circumstances in which the composition of this great poem began. Rilke was staying at a castle (Duino) on the sea near Trieste. One morning he walked out on the battlements and climbed down to where the rocks dropped sharply to the sea. If such a scene makes us think of Hamlet, about to encounter a ghost or begin a soliloquy, what follows may remind us even more of Lear, whose mind was brought to an extraordinary clarity at the brink of derangement, posing questions about human existence ("Is man no more than this? Consider him well.") while exposed to the elements. From out of the wind, which was blowing with great force, Rilke seemed to hear a voice: *Wer, wenn ich schriee, hörte mich denn aus der Engel Ordnungen?* (If I cried out, who would hear me up there, among the angelic orders?). He wrote these words, the opening of the first Duino Elegy, in his notebook, then went inside to continue what was to be his major work and one of the literary masterpieces of this century.

The story has much to tell us about poetic composition: a heightened awareness in which a voice that is and is not the poet's begins to speak, almost as if a dramatic character were reciting a "part," speaking both for himself and for all of us, as Hamlet and Lear seem to. No wonder the voice of the *Elegies* varies its pronouns so often, sometimes speaking for Rilke, sometimes to him, and, more often than not, speaking with mysterious force and urgency for and to each of us, we who are human, intrigued yet bewildered by our existence. We cannot read this great poem until we realize that it speaks in a voice at once deeply personal and piercingly

7

impersonal: Rilke's voice, Lear's voice, the voice of the wind, my voice, your voice too. To have taken the individual self, communing with itself in profound and frightening isolation, and to have made its solitary voice the every-voice that seems to respond from within us as we read the poem, was a remarkable achievement. In a sense, it reflects the aim of every lyric poem, but the peculiar tension between one self, isolated, and all selves, made one by isolation, that vibrates in the voice of this poem makes it especially dramatic. And even so, Rilke's achievement in the *Elegies* is still not fully grasped. Like the cathedrals that intrigued him, this poem has stood completed in our midst for some time now, but its clarity of outline and abundance of detail, its intimacy and majesty, are still coming into focus.

For Rilke, after that moment in the wind, it was not simply a matter of writing it down. The poem he began that day in 1912 he was to work on for ten years, an act of great artistic patience and restraint. And if the completion was troublesome, coming near the end of Rilke's life, we must also consider the effort that led up to that first outburst. Rilke had not mastered his life or his art with anything like ease. Born in Prague in 1875, he found his poetic vocation after a difficult childhood and then devoted himself to it with a dedication that cut him off from other people. Despite marriage and many friendships, he was essentially solitary, needing isolation in order to journey deeply into himself, where terror, exhilaration, and further solitude lay in wait. He forged his style slowly and with difficulty, out of nineteenth-century Romanticism and the more contemporary movements of Expressionism and Symbolism. He pressed language and imagination for a precision and an intensity that other poets still marvel at.

It was a career marked by restless travel, study, and continued uncertainty about his writing. By the time Rilke had written the *New Poems* (1907, 1908) and, more especially, *The Notebooks of Malte Laurids Brigge* (1910), an experimental prose work that resolutely explored the worst fears that memory, imagination, and existence can produce, he began to think he was artistically blocked and used up. But after two frustrating years, he found he could say, at Duino, "Solitude is a true elixir." Something was beginning to happen. He spoke of himself in letters as creeping around in the thickets of his life, "shouting like mad and clapping my hands... I howl at the moon with all my heart and put the blame on the dogs" (Lear again). But he was also poised and listening, and when the voice came on the wind he was ready: *Stimmen, Stimmen. Höre, mein Herz*...(Voices, voices. Listen, my heart...). Ten years in all it would last, that listening. A work that would combine the intensity of the lyric with the scope of the long poem, that would allow the poet to stand on the borders of life and death and sing both in anguish and jubilation, was underway at last.

\* \* \*

A student once asked me what the *Duino Elegies* were about, and before I had time to begin explaining how impossible the question was, I had already replied: "They are about what it really means to be human." I still like my thoughtless answer. The poem (or poems; it is both one and ten) resists paraphrase or identification, but that it addresses itself to what we call the human condition, with considerable force and honesty, there can be no doubt. It speaks to the distinctive and often crippling effects of our self-awareness, to the alienation from others and from ourselves that we suffer in varying degrees. It touches on children and parents, on love and lovers, on heroes and heroism, art and artists. Through its concern with this last group it deals with our attempts to use our self-consciousness to some advantage: to transcend, through art and the imagination, our self-deception and our fear.

In the process of defining and facing the terms of our existence, the poem is perhaps most famous for speaking trenchantly and courageously of death, the single overwhelming fact of mortality, the most feared and least faced aspect of our lives. Not death alone, of course, but all the things that go with it. Loss, change, pain, illness, irreparable distress. Night-fears. The ache of incessant consciousness, the cauldron of inherited savagery that steams even in children, the sense of being different from the rest of the creation, the terrifying perfection and indifference of the angel.

But these characterizations of the poem's themes suggest an abstractness that it avoids. The *Elegies* are thronged with acrobats, stories, historical characters, myths, statues, cities, landscapes, animals, carnivals, angels, words, a summer morning, dead children, and a host of astonishing metaphors. And always death, a presence, a mystery, looms up, near or far, to give the poem its fullest resonance and meaning. Rilke wrote to a Swiss friend about "the determination constantly maturing in me to keep life open towards death." To his Polish translator, he elaborated the idea:

> *Affirmation of life AND death appears as one in the 'Elegies.'* To admit the one without the other is, as is here learned and celebrated, a limitation that in the end excludes all infinity. Death is the *side of life* that is turned away from us: we must try to achieve the fullest consciousness of our existence, which is at home in the *two unseparated realms, inexhaustibly nourished by both.* . . . The true figure of life extends through *both* domains, the blood of the mightiest circulation drives through *both; there is neither a here nor a beyond, but the great unity.* . . . Transience everywhere plunges into a deep being.

Rilke's insights about the interpenetration of life and death do not account for everything the *Elegies* have to tell us, but they make an excellent starting-place for the new reader, for they mark the distinctive territory of the poem (few poets have written so searchingly about the fact and meaning of human mortality) and lead one forward, as the Lament leads the young man through the hushed land of death in the final section of the poem.

Perhaps the reader has noticed that even in explanations like the one quoted above, Rilke resorts to metaphor: nourishment, the circulation of blood, a plunge into a deep. Let this serve to remind us that the poem does not drive toward philosophical statement or toward articles of faith. Its tendency is motion, not rest, and to try to extract a system of thought from it, as readers have learned, is like nailing water or netting wind. Richard Exner spoke recently of Rilke's achievement:

> ...a new language which in turn expresses the very inseparability of intellect and emotion. After all, emotional experiences are expressed in intellectual correlatives, and the intellect interprets the emotional event!... Rilke *never* said I give you the answers. He said love the questions and perhaps you'll live your way into the answers.

There is a further lesson in metaphor. It is a unique instrument of thought, a tool, a sixth sense (or better, an extra eye, extra ear, etc.), a ladder rising from the foul rag and bone shop of the heart, a philosopher's honeymoon, an angel's mirror. And Rilke is a master of it. In an essay on Dante, the Russian poet Mandelstam provides a valuable insight into the way great poetry moves forward through sequences of metaphorical transformation:

> It is only by convention that the development of an image can be called development. Indeed, imagine to yourself an airplane (forgetting the technical impossibility) which in full flight constructs and launches another machine. In just the same way this second flying machine, completely absorbed in its own flight, still manages to assemble and launch a third. In order to make this suggestive and helpful comparison more precise, I will add that the assembly and launching of these technically unthinkable machines that are sent flying off in the midst of flight do not constitute a secondary or peripheral function of the plane that is in flight; they form a most essential attribute and part of the flight itself, and they contribute no less to its feasibility and safety than the proper functioning

of the steering gear or the uninterrupted working of
the engine.

That this description applies to Rilke's method and helps to ac-
count for the exhilaration and difficulty of his poem should be clear
to the reader before he or she is very far into the poem. It occurs
from phrase to phrase, as in the list which constitutes the answer to
Rilke's question of the angels ("Who are you?") early in the Second
Elegy. It develops from line to line and stanza to stanza, as in the
Fourth Elegy, where we career through natural images—trees,
migratory birds, lions—to the interior landscapes of lovers, to an
elaborate trope based on drawing technique, to waiting in a theater
for a performance to begin, a dancer, a puppet show, then to the
poet's relation with his father (with figures of tasting and spatial
distance) and back to the puppet show, now operated by an angel.
Perhaps most wonderful of all, this transforming process operates
from Elegy to Elegy, as the poem gathers strength and momentum
by recycling and renewing itself. One can read any Elegy by itself,
and one can browse, but to read straight through, from First to
Tenth, is to experience the full cumulative power of the transfor-
mation, the whole flight.

What of the man who made these soaring, changing figures? He
is something of a mystery. He has been worshipped and he has
been reviled. He is accused of narcissism, of inability to sustain full
relationships, of overweening egotism—these 'failings' have been
much discussed. But Rilke was no monster. He gave of himself to
others as he could, when he could, while remaining true in the way
he felt he must to his great preoccupations. Stefan Zweig, who
knew him in Paris, found himself wondering, as he wrote an
autobiography during the Second World War, whether the world
would ever again see people like Paul Valéry, Emile Verhaeren,
and Francis Jammes, artists who renounced the ephemeral and
dedicated themselves fully to their art:

> Of all these men, perhaps none lived more gently, more
> secretly, more invisibly than Rilke. But it was not will-

ful, nor forced or assumed priestly loneliness such as Stefan George celebrated in Germany; silence seemed to grow around him, wherever he went, wherever he was. Since he avoided every noise, even his own fame—that "sum of all misunderstandings, that collects itself about a name," as he once expressed it—the approaching wave of idle curiosity moistened only his name and never his person. It was difficult to reach Rilke. He had no house, no address where one could find him, no home, no steady lodging, no office. He was always on his way through the world, and no one, not even he himself, knew in advance which direction it would take.

The silence which Zweig says grew around Rilke was necessary to that extraordinary and attentive listening of the heart out of which the *Duino Elegies* began. Rilke's way through the world took him to Duino, where the poem began in 1912, and eventually to Muzot, in Switzerland, where it was completed, in a burst that included the *Sonnets to Orpheus*, in 1922. We should be grateful for that silence, that listening, that way through the world: we are their beneficiaries.

# NOTES

The first letter quoted ("Solitude... put the blame on the dogs") is to Princess Marie von Thurn und Taxis-Hohenlohe, owner of Duino, who had given him its use, and is dated December 30, 1911.

The phrase about keeping life open to death is from a letter to Nanny von Escher, December 22, 1923. Rilke's Polish translator was Witold von Hulewicz; the letter in question is dated November 13, 1925. The part of it which concerns the *Sonnets* and the *Elegies* is translated and quoted in full in M. D. Herter Norton's translation of the *Sonnets*, (Norton, 1942) pp. 131–136.

Richard Exner's lecture, "Alas, poor Rilke; His Readers, His Reception, the Boldness of Fear, and the Language of Fish," was delivered at a symposium in honor of Rilke's hundredth birthday held at Oberlin December 4–6, 1975. It later appeared, considerably expanded, as "Ach, armer Rilke! Leser und Narziss—Kühnheit der Furcht—Zeitgenossenschaft—Sprache der Fische" in *Rilke heute: Beziehungen und Wirkungen* (2. Band) Frankfurt/Main: Suhrkamp, 1976, pp. 59–94.

The translation of Mandelstam's "Talking About Dante," by Clarence Brown and Robert Hughes, was published in *Delos, 6*. The quotation is from page 81.

Stefan Zweig's autobiography, *The World of Yesterday*, was published in 1943 by Viking Press. The quotation is from page 141.

# Translator's Note

A number of translations of Rilke's *Duineser Elegien* already exist in English. None is definitive. Probably no single translation ever will be. What made me undertake the present version was a feeling that existing renderings were unsatisfactory in two ways: from the point of view of clarity, and from that of modernity. It seems to me crucial that the reader of a translation *understand* what is being said; that involves, over and over, an urgent search for the exact meaning of a passage, and, equally vital, its clear expression in the language of the translator. True "accuracy" in translation needs to be distinguished from literal sense on the one hand and loose paraphrase on the other. Literal sense fails the translator when he gives a word that has vivid associations in one language a dictionary translation into an inert, uninteresting word in the other language; the process is not at all accurate given the kind of interest that poetry brings to language. Paraphrase, if it is expressive, can be remarkably impressive when we are not in a position to question accuracy. But it invites the translator to introduce subtle (or unsubtle!) changes that withhold the unique sense of the poetic original.

When I say that a reader must understand a translation, I mean to imply as well that his interest must be aroused and held. In this respect, it seems essential to have the Elegies move with energy and sweep, carrying us forward in the current of their excitement. Too often, I felt, one could keep one's attention focused on the existing translations only with effort; like muddy rivers, they were both sluggish and unclear.

The issue of clarity is in this case intertwined with the question of modernity. Rilke began his great poem in 1912, and did not finish it until ten years later. Thus, while it belongs to a tradition and partakes of the 19th century in which the poet came to greatness, it is most definitely a poem of the modern age, a classic of this century like *The Waste Land, The Heights of Macchu Picchu, The Man With the Blue Guitar* and any of Yeats' volumes from *Responsibilities* on. Other translations seemed to me, in matters of diction, imagery, syntax and movement, too willing to face Rilke toward the past, making him sound in English like Tennyson, or Milton, or the Wordsworth of *The Prelude*. If my version seems excessively contemporary to some, it will be because I have tried to bring the poet's voice, in all its life and urgency, to the surface of the poem, free of the mufflings and wrappings of the traditional long poem in English.

The urge to achieve clarity, and the desire to let Rilke's poem speak in the voice of this century's poetry, both depended heavily, I came to feel, on a successful choice of form. As I began work on the *Elegies* I found that the long lines of the original were difficult to reproduce in English (or, more strictly speaking, American). Read aloud, they sounded fine; the listener could follow in the reader's voice the emphases, hesitations, and variations in speed. On the page, however, the long line did not readily suggest the "living" quality, and was one of the features most likely, I came to feel, to make the poem seem like a museum piece. As I was pondering solutions to this problem, I happened to re-read some of William Carlos Williams' late poetry. I realized with a start that Williams' triadic line, made up of three "variable feet," units equal in length of speaking time, was a possible model. Much of Williams' late work can with justice be called "elegiac," and his triadic line combines the comprehensiveness of the traditional elegiac line with the fragmented and eccentric qualities of modern American speech:

Inseparable from the fire
     its light
          takes precedence over it.

Then follows
    what we have dreaded—
        but it can never
overcome what has gone before.
    In the huge gap
        between the flash
and the thunderstroke
    spring has come in
        or a deep snow fallen.

A long line made up of three shorter, overlapping units makes an extremely flexible instrument of expression. The more I have worked with it, the deeper my respect for it has grown. Readers who are initially put off by having poetry "scored" so precisely on the page will find that familiarity resolves most difficulties, and that reading aloud is, as always, the best test of the poetry's efficacy. For me, moreover, the usefulness of the variable foot and the triadic line is again and again bound up with solutions not only to problems of movement and rhythmic control, but of precise expression as well, getting Rilke's difficult German to make clear and interesting sense in English. Two earlier translators of the Elegies, Edward and Vita Sackville-West, compared Rilke's line to "an immense road, admitting many thoughts and images abreast of one another, and seeming to suggest movement in more directions than one." Their solution—a monotonously regular blank verse— is dismaying, but their characterization of Rilke's line is accurate indeed, and helps, I think, to explain my choice.

One further point about my use of the "variable foot." The Elegies were serialized, as I worked on them, over a two and a half year period in the magazine FIELD. During this time my practice with the variable foot changed markedly. My first versions, I came to feel, were too choppy and fragmented, partly from an attempt to stay too close to the lines of the original. I found myself lengthening the variable foot and making it run more smoothly, and I eventually revised all ten elegies to conform to this practice. Thus, the first published version of the First Elegy was 101 lines; the present one is 82 (the original is 95). I also came to feel that normal punctuation, with the exception of commas, was most appropriate; this practice, in fact, reflects Williams' own. The present version, then, represents a fairly considerable revision of the serialized elegies, not so much in terms of phrasing (although a number of early inaccuracies have been corrected) as in line length and enjambment.

I cannot begin to document all the help and encouragement I received in the course of this project, but I am eager to acknowledge the occasional assistance I received from David Walker, Marjorie Hoover, Richard Kent, and Galway Kinnell (who made me reconsider my early handling of the triadic line), as well as the pervasive aid of John Hobbs, who read each elegy in draft and criticized it as poetry in English; of Stuart Friebert, who was characteristically generous with his time and encouragement in considering both German and English, time and again; and of Richard Exner, who urged me to a high standard of accuracy and brought his scrupulous attention to bear on all ten elegies, once through as they were serialized, and then again as I prepared the revised version, with an exemplary patience in helping me unravel the knottiest and most persistent problems. To these excellent coaches, critics, and clarifiers, I gratefully dedicate this translation.

# First Elegy

If I cried out
        who would hear me up there
                among the angelic orders?
And suppose one suddenly
        took me to his heart
                I would shrivel
I couldn't survive
        next to his
                greater existence.
Beauty is only
        the first touch of terror
                we can still bear
and it awes us so much
        because it so coolly
                disdains to destroy us.
Every single angel
        is terrible!
                And since that's the case
I choke back my own
        dark birdcall
                my sobbing.
Oh who can we turn to
        in this need?
                Not angels
not people
        and the cunning animals
                realize at once

that we aren't especially
   at home
      in the deciphered world
What's left?
    Maybe some tree
       on a hillside
one that you'd see every day
    and the perverse loyalty
       of some habit
that pleased us
    and then moved in for good.
      Oh and the night
the night, when the wind
    full of outer space
       gnaws at our lifted faces
— she'd wait for anyone
    that much desired
       mildly disappointing lady
whom the lone heart
    has to encounter
      with so much effort.
Is it easier for lovers?
    Ah, they only manage
      by being together
to conceal each other's fate!
    You *still* don't know?
      Throw armfuls of emptiness
out to the spaces
    that we breathe —
      maybe the birds
will sense
    the expanded air
      flying more fervently.

# First Elegy

Sure, spring depended on you.
>> Many stars lined up
>>> hoping you'd notice.
A wave rose toward you
>> out of the past
>>> or a violin
offered itself
>> as you passed an open window.
>>> These were instructions,
your mission.
>> But could you perform it?
>>> Weren't you always
distracted
>> waiting for something
>>> as if all this
was announcing
>> a lover's arrival?
>>> (Where could you keep her
as long as those
>> huge strange thoughts
>>> are coming and going
and staying the night?)
>> But sing, when you must,
>>> of great lovers:
their fame
>> has a long way to go
>>> before it is really immortal.
Those you almost envied
>> the unrequited
>>> whom you found
more loving
>> than the gratified
>>> the content —

begin again and again
        the praise you can never
                fully express.
Think of it:
        the hero survives.
                Even his ruin
is only another
        excuse to continue
                a final birth.
But nature, exhausted
        takes lovers
                back into herself
as if she couldn't accomplish
        that kind of vitality twice.
                Have you thought
of Gaspara Stampa
        hard enough?
                dwelt on her
so that a girl
        whose lover has disappeared
                can feel
from that tremendous
        example of love
                'Make me like her'?
Shouldn't these ancient
        sufferings of ours
                finally start to bear fruit?
Isn't it time
        that in love
                we freed ourselves
from the loved one
        and, trembling,
                endured

as the arrow endures the string
        collecting itself
                to be more than itself
as it shoots?
        For there is no remaining,
            no place to stay.


Voices, voices.
        Listen, my heart
            as only the saints
have listened
        for a gigantic call
            to lift them
right off the ground
        but they go on kneeling
            impossible beings
taking no notice
        *that's* how completely
            they listened.
Not that you
        could bear hearing
            God's voice
— oh no.
        But listen
            to that soft
blowing . . .
        that endless report
            that grows out of silence.
It rustles toward you
        from those who died young.
            When you went into churches

in Naples and Rome
        didn't their fates
                touch you gently?
Or else an inscription
        stirred you deeply
                like that tablet
in Santa Maria Formosa
        not long ago.
                What do they want of me?
I must softly erase
        my own slight
                sense of injustice
for it sometimes
        slows down
                their spirits' pure movements.


Of course it is odd
        to live no more
                on the earth
to abandon customs
        you've just begun
                to get used to
not to give meaning
        to roses
                and other such
promising things
        in terms of
                a human future
to be held no more
        by hands that can
                never relax

for fear they will drop you
      and even to put
            your name to one side
like a broken toy.
      Strange
            to wish wishes no longer.
Strange
      to see things
            that seemed to
belong together
      floating in every
            direction.
It's very hard to be dead
      and you try
            to make up for lost time
till slowly you start
      to get whiffs
            of eternity.
But the living are wrong
      in the sharp
            distinctions they make.
Angels, it seems,
      don't always know
            if they're moving among
the living or the dead.
      The drift of eternity
            drags all the ages of man
through both of those spheres
      and its sound
            rises over them both.

Those who have died young
        finally need us no longer
                — you can be weaned
from things of this world
        as gently as a child
                outgrows its mother's breast.
But we who have need
        of those huge mysteries
                we who can sometimes
draw up from
        wellsprings of sadness
                rejoicing and progress
how *could* we exist
        without them?
                Is the old tale pointless
that tells how music began
        in the midst of the mourning
                for Linos
piercing
        the arid numbness
                and, in that stunned
space
        where an almost
                godlike youth
had suddenly stopped existing
        made emptiness vibrate
                in ways
that thrill us
        comfort us
                help us now?

## Second Elegy

Every angel is terrible.
              And still, alas
                        knowing all that
I serenade you
              you almost deadly
                        birds of the soul.
Where are the days of Tobias
              when one of these
                        brightest of creatures
stood
              at the simple front door
                        disguised a little
for the trip
              and not so frightening
                        (a young man
like the one
              who looked curiously
                        out at him).
If the dangerous archangel
              took one step now
                        down toward us
from behind the stars
              our heartbeats
                        rising like thunder
would kill us.
                        Who are you?

Creation's spoiled darlings
      among the first to be perfect
           a chain of mountains
peaks and ridges
      red in the morning light
         of all creation
the blossoming godhead's pollen
      joints of pure light
           corridors
staircases
      thrones
           pockets of essence
ecstasy shields
      tumultuous storms
         of delightful feelings
then suddenly
      separate
           *mirrors*
gathering the beauty
      that streamed away from them
           back to their own faces again.


For as we feel
      we evaporate
         oh we
breathe ourselves out
      and away
           emberglow to emberglow
we give off a fainter smell.
      It's true that someone
         may say to us

'You're in my blood
   this room
     the spring
is filling with you' . . .
   What good is that?
     he can't keep us
we vanish inside him
   around him.
     And the beautiful
oh who can hold them back?
   It's endless:
     appearance shines
from their faces
   disappearing — like dew
     rising from morning grass
we breathe away
   what is ours
     like steam from a hot dish.
Oh smile where are you going?
   Oh lifted glance
     new, warm
receding wave of the heart
   woe is me?
     it's *all* of us.
Does the outer space
   into which we dissolve
     taste of us at all?
Do the angels absorb
   only what's theirs
     what streamed away from them
or do they sometimes get
   as if by mistake
     a little of our being too?

Are we mixed into
        their features
                as slightly
as that vague look
        in the faces
                of pregnant women?
In their swirling
        return to themselves
                they don't notice it.
(How could they notice it?)


Lovers, if they knew how
        might say strange things
                in the night air.
For it seems
        that all things try
                to conceal us.
See, the trees *are*
        and the houses we live in
                still hold their own,
It's just we
        who pass everything by
                like air being traded
for air.
        And all things agree
                to keep quiet about us
maybe half to shame us
        and half from a hope
                they can't express.


Lovers, you who are
        each other's satisfaction
                I ask you about us.

You hold each other.
                Does that settle it?
                        You see
it sometimes happens
                that my hands
                        grow conscious
of each other
                or that my used face
                        shelters itself
within them.
                That gives me
                        a slight sensation.
But who'd claim from that
                to *exist?*
                        You though
who grow
                by each other's ecstasy
                        until drowning
you beg 'no *more!*'
                you who under
                        each other's hands
become more abundant
                like the grapes
                        of great vintages
fading at times
                but only because
                        the other completely
takes over —
                I ask you about us.
                        I know
that touch
                is a blessing for you
                        because the caress lasts

because what you cover
      so tenderly
            does not disappear
because you can sense
      underneath the touch
            some kind of pure
duration.
      Somehow eternity
            almost seems possible
as you embrace.
      And yet
            when you've got past
the fear in that first
      exchange of glances
            the mooning at the window
and that first walk
      together in the garden
            *one time:*
lovers, *are* you the same?
      When you lift
            each other to your lips
mouth to mouth
      drink to drink —
            oh how oddly
the drinker seems
      to withdraw
            from the act of drinking.


Weren't you astonished
      by the discretion
            of human gesture

on Attic grave steles?
　　　　Didn't love and parting
　　　　　　　sit so lightly
on shoulders
　　　　that they seemed
　　　　　　　to be made of a substance
different from ours?
　　　　Do you recall
　　　　　　　how the hands rest
without any pressure
　　　　though there is great
　　　　　　　strength in the torsos?
Those figures spoke
　　　　a language of self-mastery:
　　　　　　　we've come to this point
this is us
　　　　touching this way
　　　　　　　the gods
may push us around
　　　　but that is something
　　　　　　　for them to decide.
If only we too
　　　　could discover an orchard
　　　　　　　some pure, contained
human, narrow
　　　　strip of land
　　　　　　　between river and rock.
For our own heart
　　　　outgrows us
　　　　　　　just as it did them
and we can't follow it
　　　　by gazing at pictures
　　　　　　　that soothe it

or at godlike bodies
      that restrain it
           by their very size.

## Third Elegy

It's one thing
            to sing the beloved.
                        That hidden
guilty river-god
            of the blood
                        is something else.
What does her young lover
            whom she can recognize
                        at a distance
understand of that
            lord of desire, who often
                        out of this lonely young man
(before the girl soothed him
            and often as if
                        she didn't exist)
raised his godhead
            dripping with what
                        unrecognizable stuff
rousing the night
            to a continuous
                        tumult.
Oh Neptune of the blood
            his terrible trident.
                        Oh the dark wind
sounding from his chest
            through the spiral conch!
                        Listen to the night

scooping and hollowing out . . .
>> You stars
>>>> doesn't the lover's
delight in his
>> loved one's countenance
>>>> come from you?
Doesn't his secret insight
>> into her pure face
>>>> come from the pure constellations?


It wasn't you
>> oh no
>>>> and it wasn't his mother
who bent his brows
>> to this expectant arch.
>>>> Not from your mouth
girl so aware of him
>> not from that contact
>>>> did his lips curve
into this fruitful expression.
>> Do you really think
>>>> your soft approach
could shake him that way
>> you who walk
>>>> like the wind at dawn?
Oh yes you startled
>> his heart
>>>> but more ancient fears
crashed down inside him
>> at the shock of your touch.
>>>> Call him . . .

you can't free him
            completely from
                        those dark companions.
Of course he *wants* to escape
            and he does
                        and relieved he gets used to
your heart's seclusion
            and takes hold
                        and begins to be himself.
But did he
            ever really
                        begin himself?
Mother
            *you* made him little
                        you started him
he was new to you
            and you arched
                        the friendly world
over his new eyes
            and shut out
                        the strange one.
Where, where
            are the years
                        when your slender shape
was simply enough
            to block out
                        waves of approaching chaos?
You hid so much from him this way
            rendering harmless
                        the room that grew
suspicious at night
            and from the full
                        sanctuary of your heart

you mixed something human
      into his nightspace.
            And you set the night-light
not in the darkness
      but in your nearness
           your presence
and it shone
      out of friendship.
           There wasn't a creak
you couldn't explain
      smiling
           as if you had known
for a long time
      *exactly* when
           the floor would assert itself . . .
And he listened
      and he was soothed.
           That's what your
getting up
      so tenderly
           achieved: his tall
cloaked fate went back
      behind the wardrobe
           and his unruly future
(so easily mussed)
      conformed to the folds
           of the curtain.


And while he lay there
      relieved
           with your image

dissolving sweetly
       under his drowsy lids
              as he sank towards sleep
he *seemed* protected . . .
       but *within*
              who could divert
or contain
       the floods
              of his origin?
Ah, there *were*
       no precautions in the sleeper
              . . . sleeping
but dreaming, but
       running a fever
              how he let himself go!
He, the new one
       the shy one
              how he was tangled
in the spreading
       roots and tendrils
              of inner event
twisting in primitive patterns
       in choking growths
              in the shapes
of killer animals.
       How he submitted.
       Made love.
Loved his own
       inwardness
              his inner wilderness
the primeval forest
       where his heart stood
              like a green shoot

among huge fallen trees.
            Made love.
                        Let it go, went on
down through his own
            roots and out
                        to the monstrous beginning
where his little birth
            had happened so long ago.
                        Loving it
he waded downward
            into more ancient blood
                        into canyons
where Horror itself
            lay gorged from eating
                        his fathers
and every Terror
            knew him
                        and winked in complicity.

Yes, Atrocity smiled . . .
            seldom had you
                        smiled that tenderly, mother.
Why shouldn't he love it
            since it had smiled.
                        He loved it
*before* he loved you
            because when you carried him
                        it was already
dissolved
            in the water that makes
                        the embryo float.


You see
            we don't love
                        a single season

like the flowers.
         When we love
              a sap
older than time
         rises through our arms.
            My dear
it's like this:
         that we love *inside* ourselves
            not one person
not some future being
         but seething multitudes
            not a particular child
but the fathers
         who lie at rest
            in our depths
like ruined mountains
         and the dry riverbeds
            of earlier mothers
and the whole
         soundless landscape
            under the clouded
or clear sky
         of its destiny
            *this*, my dear
came before you.


And you yourself
         what do you know?
            You stirred up
prehistory
         in your lover.
            What passions

welled up
> from those long dead beings?
>> What women

hated you
> what kind of men
>> lost in darkness

did you waken within
> his youthful veins?
>> Dead children

strained to touch you . . .
> Oh gently, gently
>> do a loving day's work

for his sake
> lead him
>> toward the garden

let him have
> more than enough of the night . . .

> Hold him back . . .

## Fourth Elegy

O trees of life
           when is your winter?
                       We're not in tune
we're not instinctive
           like migrating birds.
                      Overtaken
overdue
           we push ourselves suddenly
                  into the wind
and arrive surprised
           at an indifferent pond.
                  We understand
blooming and withering
           we know them both at once.
                  And somewhere lions roam
knowing nothing of weakness
           so long as their
                  majesty lasts.


But we
           when we're fully intent
                  on one thing
can already feel
           the pull of another.
                  Hatred is always close by.

Aren't lovers always
        coming to sheer drop-offs
                inside each other
they who promised themselves
        open spaces, good hunting
                and a homeland?
As when for some
        quick sketch
                a contrasting background
is made with great care
        so we can see the drawing.
                No effort is spared.
We don't know
        the contour of feeling
                we only know what molds it
from without.
        Who hasn't sat tense
                before his own heart's curtain?
It rose.
        There was the scenery
            of departure.
Easy to understand.
        The familiar garden
            swaying slightly.
Then the dancer appeared.
        Not *him*! Enough!
                However lightly he moves
he's just disguised
        and he turns into a burgher
            who enters his house
by way of the kitchen.
        I don't want these
            half-filled masks

a doll, a puppet
        is better. It's full.
                I can endure
the stuffed body
        and the wire
                and the face that's
pure appearance.
        Here. I'm waiting.
                Even if the lights go out
even if they tell me
        "That's all"
                even if emptiness
drifts from the stage
        in gray puffs of air
                even if none
of my silent ancestors
        sits by me any more
                no woman
not even the boy
        with the brown squinting eye.
                I'll stay put anyway.
I can still watch.


Don't you think I'm right?
        You, father
                whose life
tasted so bitter
        after you tasted mine
                the first thick doses
of my necessity
        still tasting
                again and again

as I grew up
        and, intrigued
                by the aftertaste
of such a strange future
        tried out my cloudy gaze
                you, my father
who so often since
        your own death
                have had fears about me
deep in my own hope
        giving up that calm
                that the dead have
surrendering
        whole kingdoms of calm
                for my morsel of fate.
Don't you think I'm right?
        And you
                don't you think so?
you who loved me
        for my little beginning
                of love for you
I always lost track of
        because the distance
                in your face
even as I loved it
        turned into outer space
                where you no longer existed . . .
When I'm in the mood
        to wait
                in front of the puppet stage
no, rather to stare
        so intently that finally
                an angel must come

as an actor
        to make up for my staring
                pulling the stuffed bodies
up to life.
        Angel and puppet:
                then at last
there's a play.
        Then what we separate
                by our very being
comes together.
        Then the whole
                cycle of change
finds its first origin
        in the seasons of our life.
                Above us then
and just beyond
        the angel is playing.
                Look, surely the dying
should guess how full
        of pretence everything
                we achieve here is.
Nothing is really itself.
        Oh the hours in childhood
                when the shapes of things
spoke of more than the past
        and when what lay before us
                wasn't the future.
We grew of course
        and we sometimes hurried
                to grow up sooner
half for the sake of those
        who had nothing more
                than the fact

of being grown up.
          Yet we contented ourselves
                    in our solitary play
with permanent things
          and we stood there
                    in the gap
between world and plaything
          in a place that had been
                    prepared from the start
for some pure event.


Who shows a child
          as he really is?
                    Who sets him among the stars
and puts the measure of distance
          in his hand?
                    Who makes the child's death
out of gray bread
          that gets hard
                    who leaves it there
in his round mouth
          like the core
                    of a lovely apple?
Murderers aren't hard
          to comprehend.
                    But this:
to contain death
          the whole of death
                    even *before* life has begun
to contain it so gently
          and not to be angry —
                    this is indescribable.

# Fifth Elegy

*dedicated to Frau Hertha von Koenig*

But tell me
>who *are* they
>>these vagabonds
even more transient
>than we are?
>>urged on from childhood
twisted (for whose sake?)
>by some will
>>that is never content?
Instead it keeps
>twisting them
>>bending them
slings them and
>swings them
>>tosses them up
and catches them
>they seem to come down
>>from an oiled and
slipperier air
>to land on a carpet
>>worn threadbare
from their continual
>leaping and tumbling
>>a carpet lost in the cosmos

stuck there like a plaster
        as if the suburban sky
                had somehow wounded the earth.
And barely there
        upright, showing faintly
                the huge capital D
that seems to stand
        for existence . . . presence . . .
                the relentless grip
rolls even the strongest men
        round and round
                having fun
like Augustus the Strong
        **rolling a tin plate up**
                at the dinner table.


Ah, and around this center:
        the rose of watching
                blooming
and dropping its petals.
        Around this pestle
                this pistil
smitten by its own
        blossoming pollen
                re-fertilized to bear
the false fruit of disgust
        that they're never conscious of
                the glossiest veneer
lit by the smirk of disgust.


There's the limp
        wrinkled
                weight-lifter

an old man who now
         just beats the drum
                  shrunk in his
mighty skin
         as if it had once
                  held *two* men
and the other
         already lay
                  in the graveyard
while this one
         survived him
                  living on, deaf
and sometimes
         a bit dazed in his widowed
                  skin.
But the young one, the man
         who might be the son
                  of a neck and a nun
tightly and powerfully filled
         with muscle
                  and artlessness.


Oh you, all of you
         who were given
                  to be the toy
of some pain
         when it was still young
                  during one of its long
convalescences . . .


And you especially
         who fall daily
                  a hundred times

unripe, with the plummet
        that only fruit can know
                from that tree
of jointly constructed motion
        (that goes through
                spring, summer
and autumn
        in a few minutes
                faster than water)
fall with a thump
        on the grave:
                sometimes
in a split-second pause
        a loving look
                toward your
seldom tender mother
        may start to rise up
                in your face:
then it loses itself
        in your body
                whose surface absorbs it
that self-conscious
        hardly attempted look
                and again
the man claps his hands
        for your leap
                and before
any pain can get closer
        to your heart
                that is always
galloping on ahead
        there comes that burning
                in the soles of your feet

anticipating what causes it
   and chasing a few
      quick physical tears
into your eyes.
   And still, blindly
      the smile . . .


O take it, angel!
   pluck it
      this small-flowered
healing herb
   and go get a vase for it
      preserve it!
Put it with those joys
   **that *still* aren't**
      open to us
praise it
   in a lovely urn
      with a florid
soaring inscription:
      *Subrisio*
      *Saltat.*
 And then you
   darling, you
      whom the most
delicious pleasures
   have leaped right over
      silently.
Maybe your frills
   are happy for you —
      or the green

metallic silk
        tight across
                your hard young breasts
feels that it's
        endlessly pampered
                and in need of nothing.
You
        set out on display
                again and again
but differently each time
        like the indifferent fruit
                on the wavering
pans of the balance
        in public
                below the shoulders.


Where, oh *where*
        is that place
                — I carry it in my heart —
where for a long time
        they *couldn't* perform
                but fell away from each other
like mating animals
        badly paired
                where the weights
are still heavy
        where the plates
                still wobble off
the fruitlessly
        twirling sticks . . .

And suddenly
        in this difficult Nowhere
                suddenly the ineffable
place where the pure
        "Too-little"
                incredibly transforms itself
somersaulting
        into that empty
                "Too-much."
Where the problem that had
        so many digits
                comes out right
with nothing left over.


Squares
        oh square in Paris
                infinite showplace
where the milliner
        Madame Lamort
                slings and winds
the restless
        ways of the world
                endless ribbons
finding new loops for them
        frill flowers
                cockades
artificial fruits
        — all falsely dyed
                for the cheap winter hats
of Destiny.

  .   .   .   .   .   .   .   .   .   .   .   .   .   .

Angel: suppose there's a place
            we don't know of
                        and there
on an indescribable carpet
            lovers could show
                        the feats they aren't
able to show here
            the daring high figures
                        of the heart's leap
their towers of ecstasy
            their ladders long since
                        propped against each other
where there was never any ground
            trembling
                        and they *could*
before the surrounding
            spectators, the hushed
                        innumerable dead:
wouldn't those dead
            throw them then
                        their forever hoarded
and hidden
            unknown to us
                        but eternally current
coins of happiness
            at the feet of the pair
                        whose smile was finally
truthful there
            on that fulfilled
                        carpet?

## Sixth Elegy

Fig tree
      for a long time
            it's meant a lot to me
how you almost completely
      skip blossoming
            and press your purest secret
unglorified
      ahead of time
            into your definite fruit.
Like the pipe
      of a fountain
            your arching boughs
drive the sap down
      drive it up
            and it springs from sleep
hardly awake
      to the joy of its
            sweetest achievement.
See:
      like the god
            into the swan.


                  . . . But we
we linger, alas
      our honor lies
            in our blooming

and we're betrayed
        by the time we enter
                the overdue core
of our ultimate fruit.
        Only for a few
                the urge to action
rises so strongly
        that they're already
                standing by
glowing
        in the fullness of their hearts
                when the temptation to bloom
touches their young mouths
        and eyelids
                like soothing night air:
heroes, maybe
        and those who are meant
                to disappear early
whose veins
        Death the gardener
                has twisted differently.
They hurtle ahead
        in advance of their own smiles
                like the team
of charging horses
        before the conquering king
                in the mild, molded reliefs
at Karnak.



The hero is strangely close
        to those who died young.
                Permanence

doesn't interest him.
        His dawn is his lifetime.
           He constantly
takes himself off
        and enters
           the changed constellation
of his everlasting risk.
        Few could find him there.
           But that dark Fate
who has nothing to say for us
        suddenly all inspired
           sings him on into the storm
of his uproarious world.
        I hear no one like him.
           All at once
his dimmed note
        carried on rivering air
           sounds through me.


Then how I'd like to hide
        from this great longing!
           If I were, oh
if I were a boy
        and still had the chance
           still sat
arms propped on the future
        and read about Samson
           how his mother gave birth
to nothing and then
        to everything.
           Wasn't he hero already
inside you, mother
        and didn't his
           imperious choosing

begin there within you?
        Thousands were brewing
                in the womb
wishing to be *him*
        but look:
                he took hold
he discriminated
        chose and accomplished.
                And if he ever
broke pillars apart
        it was when he burst out
                of the world of your body
into a narrower world
        where he went on
                choosing, accomplishing.
Oh mothers of heroes!
        sources of such
                torrential rivers!
You gorges in which
        virgins have already
                plunged, weeping
from the heart's high rim
        future offerings
                to the son.


For whenever the hero
        stormed through the stations of love
                each heart that beat
for his sake
        only lifted him higher
                and, already turning away
he stood
        at the end of the smiles
                transformed.

## Seventh Elegy

No more wooing, voice
    you're outgrowing that
        don't let your cry
be a wooing cry
    even though it could be
        as pure as a bird's
that the season lifts up
    as she herself rises
        nearly forgetting
that it's just
    a fretful creature
        and not some single heart
to be tossed
    toward happiness
        deep into intimate skies.
Like him you want
    to call forth a still
        invisible mate
a silent listener
    in whom a reply
        slowly awakens
warming itself
    by hearing yours
        to become
your own
    bold feeling's
        blazing partner.

Oh and spring
        would understand
                — not one crevice
that wouldn't echo
        annunciation.
                The first small
questioning flutenotes
        reinforced by echoing stillness
                that rises all round
in the pure, affirmative day.
        Then on up the steps —
                a call that climbs
each air-stair
        toward the dreamed
                temple of the future
then the trill
        the fountain
                whose rising jet
catches the falling water
        up again
                in a game of promising . . .
And all before it
        the Summer.
                Not only those
summer mornings
        not only the way
                they change into day
glowing because of the sunrise.
        Not only the days
                gentle among the flowers
while strong and enormous
        overhead, among the great
                shapes of the trees.

Not only the devotion
      of these unfolded powers
            not only the roads
not only the evening meadows
      not only the clear breathing
            that follows afternoon thunderstorms
not only approaching sleep
      and a premonition
            late evening . . .
But the nights!
      but the high summer nights
            but the stars
stars of the earth.
      Oh to be dead
            one of these days
and to know that *they*
      are infinite
            all of the stars
for how
      how
            how to forget them!


You see, I've called for a lover.
      But it wasn't just she
            who would come.
Girls would come out of
      inadequate graves
            and stand near . . .
Well how could I
      limit my call
            after I'd called it?

The buried are always
        seeking the earth again.
                You children
one single thing
        fully grasped
                here and now
would be valid
        for many.
                Don't suppose
that fate's any more
        than childhood's density.
                How often you really
overtook your lover
        breathing, breathing deep
                after a marvelous run
toward nothing more
        than the open air.


Just to *be* here
        is a delight!
                You knew that too
you girls who seemed
        deprived of it
                you who were sunk
in the city's worst alleys
        festering there, or exposed
                to its garbage and filth.
For each had an hour
        or maybe not even that much
                just some unmeasurable

moment of time
        between two whiles
                when she had existence
completely
        down to her fingertips!
                It's just that we forget
so easily
        what our genial neighbor
                neither approves of
nor grudges us.
        We want it visible
        to show
when even the most
        visible joy
                will reveal itself
only when we have
        transformed it within.


There's nowhere, my love
        the world can exist
                except within.
Our lives are used up
        in transformations
                and what's outside us
always diminishing
        vanishes.
                Where a solid house
once stood
        a wholly fictitious image
                cuts in, just as if

the whole thing existed
            completely in the brain.
                        The Zeitgeist creates
huge silos of power
            that are as shapeless
                        as the straining urge
he acquires from everything else.
            He has forgotten the temples.
                        We are the ones
who try surreptitiously
            to save such squanderings
                        of the heart.
Yes, where one still stands
            a thing that once was
                        prayed to, knelt to,
served — it reaches
            just as it is
                        into the unseen world.
Many don't notice
            and miss the chance
                        to build it now
*inside* themselves
            with pillars and statues
                        greater than ever!


Every heavy
            turning back of the earth
                        has such disinherited ones
who possess
            neither earlier things
                        nor what's to come.

For what's ahead
>> is distant for men.
>>>> This shouldn't confuse *us*
it should confirm
>> our preserving a form
>>>> we still recognize:
This *stood* among men
>> at one time
>>>> stood in the midst of fate
of destructive fate
>> stood in the midst of not
>>>> knowing where to go
as if it existed
>> and bent the stars
>>>> down toward it
from the established heavens.
>> Angel!
>>>> I'm showing it to you
*there it is*!
>> let it stand
>>>> so that you see it
redeemed at last
>> upright.
>>>> Columns, pylons,
the Sphinx
>> the cathedral's gray
>>>> determined thrust
from some fading
>> or unknown city.


>>>> Wasn't this like a miracle?

Gaze at it, angel
　　　　it's *us*
　　　　　　　　you mighty being
you tell them that we could
　　　　accomplish such things
　　　　　　　　my breath isn't enough
for such celebration.
　　　　　　For it seems after all
　　　　　　　　that we haven't neglected
the spaces
　　　　our generous portion
　　　　　　　　these spaces — *ours*
(How frighteningly vast
　　　　they must be
　　　　　　　　if thousands of years
of our feelings
　　　　have not overcrowded them. )
　　　　　　　　But a tower was great
wasn't it?
　　　　Oh angel it was
　　　　　　it was great
even set next to you.
　　　　Chartres was great
　　　　　　　　and music reached
even higher
　　　　climbing beyond us.
　　　　　　　　Even a girl in love
alone at night
　　　　by her window
　　　　　　　　didn't she reach to your knee?

Don't think I'm wooing you!
        Angel
                even if I am
you won't come
        for my call
                is always full of rising
you can't move
        against such a current
                it's just too strong.
My call is an outstretched arm
        and its high, reaching
                open hand
is always before you
        open
                incomprehensible being
wide open
        to defend
                to warn off.

# *Eighth Elegy*

*dedicated to Rudolf Kassner*

With its whole gaze
        a creature
                looks out at the open.
But our eyes
        are as though turned in
                and they seem to set traps
all around it
        as if to prevent
                its going free.
We can only know
        what *is* out there
                from an animal's features
for we make even infants
        turn and look back
                at the way things are shaped
not toward the open
        that lies so deep
                in an animal's face.
Free from death.
        Because we're the ones
                who see death.
The animal that's free
        always has
                its destruction behind it

and God ahead of it
        and when it moves
                it moves forward
forever and ever
        like a flowing spring.


                *We* never have
even for one single day
        that pure space before us
                that flowers can open
endlessly into.
        It's always *world*
                it's never a nowhere
where there isn't
        any 'no,' any 'don't'
                never the pure
the untended thing
        you breathe
                and endlessly *know*
and never desire:
        what a child
                sometimes gives himself up to
and grows still
        and has to be
                shaken out of.
Or another one dies
        and then *is* it.
                For when you get close to death
you don't see death anymore
        you look out *past* it
                and maybe then

with an animal's wide gaze.
        Lovers, if they weren't
                blocking each other's view
are close to it
        marveling . . .
                As if by an oversight
it opens up to them
        behind each other . . .
                But neither one can get past
and again
        world comes back to them.
                Always when we face
the creation
        we see only
                a kind of reflection
of the freedom
        that we ourselves have dimmed.
                Or it happens
that an animal
        some mute beast
                raises its head
and imperturbably
        looks right through us.
                That's what fate means:
to be facing each other
        and nothing but each other
                and to be doing it forever.


If the animal
        coming toward us so surely
                from another direction

had our kind of consciousness
he'd drag us around in his sway.
But his being

is infinite to him
incomprehensible, and without
a sense of his condition

pure as his gaze.
And where we see the future
he sees everything

and himself *in* everything
healed and whole
forever.


And yet within
the warm and watchful beast
there's the weight and care

of a huge sadness.
For there clings to him
something that often

overwhelms us
— memory
a recollection that

whatever we're striving for now
was once closer and truer
and that its union with us

was incredibly tender.
Here everything is distance
there it was breath.

After the first home
the second seems hybrid
and windy.

Oh the bliss
        of the *little* creature
                that *stays* forever
inside the womb that conceived it.
        Oh happiness of the gnat
                still hopping *within*
even on its wedding day:
        for womb
                is everything.
And look at the
        half assurance of the bird
                that almost seems to know
both states from his origin
        like the soul of an Etruscan
                come from a dead man
stowed in a space
        with his own resting figure
                as the lid.
And how bewildered
        is something that has to fly
                if it came from a womb.
As though.terrified of itself
        it shivers through the air
                the way a crack
goes through a cup
        the way a bat's track tears
                through the porcelain of evening.


And we:
        spectators, always
                everywhere

looking at all of that
        never beyond!
               It fills us too full.
We set it right.
        It disintegrates.
               We set it right again
and we disintegrate too.


Who has turned us around this way
        so that we're always
               whatever we do
in the posture of someone
        who is leaving?
               Like a man
on the final hill
        that shows him
               his whole valley
one last time
        who turns and stands there
               lingering —
that's how we live
        always
               saying goodbye.

## Ninth Elegy

Why, if it's possible
    to spend our little
        span of existence
as laurel
    slightly darker
        than all the other greens
with tiny waves
    on each leaf's rim
        (like a wind's smile)
— why then
    still insist
        on being human
and shrinking from fate
    long for it too? . . .

        Oh, not because happiness
— that part of approaching ruin
    that rushes ahead of it —
        is *real.*
Not out of curiosity
    not to exercise the heart
        that would have been fine
in the laurel . . .
    But just because to be here
        means so much

and because
        everything here
                **all this that's disappearing**
seems to need us
        to concern us
                in some strange way
we, who disappear
        even faster!
                It's *one* time
for each thing
        and *only* one.
                Once and no more.
And the same for us:
        *once.*
                Then never again.
But this once having been
        even though only once
                having been *on earth*
seems as though
        it can't be undone.


And so we push ourselves
        wanting to master it
                wanting to hold it all
in our own two hands
        in the overloaded gaze
                and the dumbstruck heart.
Trying to become it.
        To give it to someone?
                No, we'd like most

to keep it all ourselves
   forever . . .
     Ah, but what
can we take across
   to the other realm
     when we leave?
Not our perception
   learned here so slowly
     and nothing
that's happened here.
   Not one thing.
     So that means we take pain.
Take, above all
   the heaviness of existing
     take the long
experience of love
   take
     truly unsayable things.
But later
   under the stars
     why bother?
They are *better*
   at the unsayable.
     After all, isn't what
the wanderer brings back
   from the mountain slopes
     to the valley
not a handful of earth
   that no one could *say*
     but rather a word
hard-won, pure,
   the yellow and blue
     gentian?

Are we on this earth to say:
        House
               Bridge
Fountain
      Jug        Gate
               Fruit-tree       Window
at best:
        Column . . .
               Tower . . .?
but to *say* these words
      you understand
            with an intensity
the things themselves
      never dreamed they'd express.
            Isn't the earth's
hidden strategy
      when she so slyly
            urges two lovers on
that each and every thing
      should be transformed
            by the delight
of sharing their feelings?

        Threshold:


what it means
      to two lovers
            that they too
should be wearing down
      an old doorsill
           a bit more

after the many
   before them
     and before
the many to come
     . . . lightly.


*Here* is the time
   for the *sayable*
     here is its home.
Speak, bear witness.
   More than ever
     things fall away from us
livable things
   and what crowds them out
     and replaces them
is an event
   for which there's no image.
     An event
under crusts
   that will tear open
     easily
just as soon
   as it outgrows them
     and its interests
call for new limits.
   Between the hammer strokes
     our hearts survive
like the tongue
   that between the teeth
     and in spite of everything
goes on praising.

Praise the world
        to the angel
                not the unsayable
you can't impress him
        with sumptuous feelings —
                in the universe
where he feels things
        so fully
                you're just a novice.
Show him, then,
        some simple thing
                shaped by its passage
through generations
        that lives as a belonging
                near the hand, in the gaze.
Tell him of Things.
        He'll stand more astonished
                than you did
beside the rope-maker
        in Rome, or the potter
                by the Nile.
Show him how happy
        a thing can be
                how blameless and ours
how even the wail of sorrow
        can settle purely
                into its own form
and serve as a thing
        or die into a thing
                to a realm where even
the violin can't recall it.
        And these things
                that take their life

from impermanence
        they understand
                that you're praising them:
perishing, they trust
        to us — the most
                perishable of all —
for their preservation.
        They want us to change them
                completely
inside our invisible hearts
        into — oh endlessly —
                into ourselves!
Whoever we might
        turn out to be
                at the end.


Earth, isn't this
        what you want:
                rising up
inside us *invisibly*
        once more?
                Isn't it your dream
to be invisible someday?
        Earth! invisible!
                what is it
you urgently ask for
        if not transformation?
                Earth, my love
I will do it.
        Believe me
                your springtimes

are no longer needed
　　　　to win me — *one*
　　　　　　　　just one, is already
too much for my blood.
　　　　I have been yours
　　　　　　　　unable to say so
for a long time now.
　　　　You were right
　　　　　　　　always
and affable Death
　　　　is your own
　　　　　　　　holy notion.


Look, I'm living.
　　　　On what?
　　　　　　　　Neither my childhood
nor my future
　　　　is growing smaller . . .
　　　　　　　　Being
in excess
　　　　wells up
　　　　　　　　in my heart.

# Tenth Elegy

That someday
        at the close of this
                fierce vision
I might sing praise
        and jubilation to
                assenting angels.
That the heart's
        clear-striking hammers
                might not falter
from landing on
        slack or doubtful
                or snapping strings.
That my face, streaming
        might make me
                more radiant
that this homely weeping
        might bloom.
                Oh you nights
that I grieved through
        how much you will
                mean to me then.
Disconsolate sisters
        why didn't I kneel
                more fully
to accept you
        and lose myself more
                in your loosened hair?

How we squander our sorrows
        gazing beyond them
                into the sad
wastes of duration
        to see if maybe
                they have a limit.
But they are
        our winter foliage
                our dark evergreens
*one* of the seasons
        of our secret year
                — and not only a season
they are situation,
        settlement, lair,
                soil, home.


It's true, though:
        how strange are the back streets
                of Pain City
where, in the false silence
        created from too much noise
                there swaggers out
the slop that's cast
        from the mould of emptiness
                the gilded hubbub
the bursting monument.
        Oh how an angel
                would stamp out their
Consolation Market
        leaving no trace
                — the church beside it too

bought ready-made
           as swept and shut tight
                     and disappointed
as a post office
           on Sunday.
                     Out further, though
there are always
           the rippling edges of the Fair.
                     Freedom's swing-rides!
Zeal's divers and jugglers!
           And tarted-up Good Luck's
                     lifelike shooting range
where the tin targets
           ring and flop over
                     when a better shot hits them.
From cheer to chance
           he lurches on
                     since booths
to please all curiosities
           babble and drum
                     and tout their wares.
Special Attraction for Adults:
           How Money Reproduces
                     Anatomically Valid
Not Just Entertainment
           Money's Own Genitals
                     Nothing Left Out
The Act Itself
           It's Educational
                     and It Helps
Make You Potent . . .
           Oh, but just outside
                     beyond the last

billboard plastered
        with ads for "Deathless"
                that bitter beer
that tastes sweet
        to its drinkers
                as long as they keep chewing
fresh distractions —
        just behind that billboard
                right there
everything's *real.*
        Children play there
                and lovers embrace
off to one side
        so seriously
                in the sparse grass
where dogs do doggy things.
        The young man is drawn
                further — maybe he's fallen
in love with a young Lament . . .
        He follows her into the meadows
                she says:
It's a long way.
        We live out there . . .
                Where?
And the young man follows.
        Roused by the way she moves.
                Her shoulder, her neck —
maybe she comes from
        a splendid race.
                But he leaves her
goes back, turning
        to wave . . . What's the use?
                She's just a Lament.

Only those who've died young
        in their first state
                of timeless calm
— their weaning —
        follow her lovingly.
                She waits for young girls
and befriends them.
        Gently she shows them
                what she wears.
Pearls of pain
        and the fine-spun
                veils of Patience.
With young men
        she walks along
                in silence.


But there where they live
        in the valley
                one of the older Laments
answers the youth
        when he questions her:
                We were once
she says,
        a great race
                we Laments.
Our fathers
        worked the mines up there
                in the mountain-range
sometimes among men
        you'll find a polished
                lump of primeval Pain

or the petrified slag
          of Anger from
                    an old volcano.
Yes, that came from up there.
          We used to be rich.


And she leads him lightly
          through the broad
                    landscape of Lamentation
shows him the columns of temples
          or the ruins of castles
                    from which the Lords of Lament
once ruled the land wisely.
          Shows him the tall tear trees
                    and the fields of sadness in bloom
(what the living know only
          as tender foliage)
                    shows him the herds of grief
pasturing
          and sometimes
                    a bird startles
and writes
          as it flies flatly
                    through their field of vision
the image of its
          solitary cry.
                    In the evening
she leads him to the graves
          of the ancients
                    of the race of Laments
the sibyls
          and the lords of warning.
                    But when night comes

they go more slowly
   and soon there looms ahead
      in the moonlight
the sepulcher
   that watches over everything.
      Twin brother
to the one on the Nile
   the tall Sphinx
      the silent chamber's
countenance.
   And they marvel
      at the regal head
that has silently
   and forever
      set the human face
to be weighed
   on the scale
      of the stars.


His sight, still dizzy
   from early death
      can't grasp it.
But hers
   frightens the owl
      from behind the rim
of the crown.
   And the bird
      brushing with slow
downstrokes
   along the cheek
      — the one

with the roundest curve —
        inscribes faintly
                on the new sense of hearing
that follows death
        an indescribable outline
                as if on the doubly opened
page of a book.


And higher up, the stars.
        New ones.
                Stars of the Painlands.
Slowly, the Lament
        tells him their names:
                "Here — look:
the Rider
        the Staff
                and that dense constellation
they call the Fruitgarland.
        Then further up
                toward the Pole:
the Cradle, the Path
        the Burning Book
                the Puppet, the Window.
But in the southern sky
        pure as within the palm
                of a consecrated hand
the clear, shining M
        that stands for the Mothers . . . ."


But the dead man
        must go on
                and silently

the older Lament
        takes him as far as the gorge
                where the spring
the source of Joy
        shimmers in moonlight.
                She names it with reverence
saying:
        "In the world of men
            this is a life-bearing stream."


They stand
        at the foot
            of the mountain
and there
        she embraces him
            crying.


Alone, he goes off climbing
        into the mountains
            of primal Pain.
And not even
        his footstep
            rings from this soundless fate.


Yet if these
        endlessly dead
            awakened a simile for us
look, they might point
        to the catkins
            hanging from empty hazeltrees

or else they might mean the rain
            that falls on the dark earth
                        in spring.


And we
            who always think
                        of happiness *rising*
would feel the emotion
            that almost startles us
                        when a happy thing *falls*.

# Notes and Comments

## First Elegy

The traditional beginning of a long poem is an invocation, asking for help from a divine source, a muse. Rilke's is the opposite, a turning away, a refusal. The poet is on his own, considering what poetry can be without supernatural sanctions. But if the poet cannot expect contact with angels, he must nevertheless be attentive to the fact and meaning of death. The invocation gradually takes the form of a willingness, even a desire, to listen to what the dead have to tell us. The distinctions between death and life are re-examined. If the dead do not need us, we begin to realize, we do need them. Music, for example, had its origin in the ancient experience of grief.

*angelic orders:* Rilke's angels, as the poem makes clear, are not those of Christian orthodoxy. He once noted that they were more like those of Islam. The best definition of them remains the poem itself.

*Gaspara Stampa:* an Italian poet of the 16th Century. Abandoned by her lover, she responded not with despair but by writing poetry and venturing into other love affairs. She died at the age of thirty-one.

*Santa Maria Formosa:* a church in Venice Rilke had visited in 1911.

*Linos:* a vegetation god similar to Adonis. It seems likely that Rilke supposed his mourner to be Orpheus, the legendary first poet and musician. It is as though the first experience of grief produced the first music.

## Second Elegy

The poem's tendency to use motifs both of image and idea is clear as Rilke again takes up the matter of contact with the angels. This time, though, the focus is not so much the role of the poet as the meaning of our mutability, our ephemeral place in the world. Lovers seem to be in touch with a more lasting existence, a greater reality, but they cannot sustain it. Greek funerary sculpture (*steles* are stone slabs carved in relief) shows, in its dignity and restraint, an acceptance of human transience, and we need an equivalent that we can't seem to find in today's pictures or statuary.

*Tobias:* in the apocryphal Book of Tobit, the angel Raphael guides Tobias, who does not recognize him, on a difficult journey.

## Third Elegy

The exploration of love continues, and a new motif, that of the child, makes its appearance. Again, we seem to have an equivalent to a traditional feature of the epic: the descent to the underworld. Here the journey is interior, reflecting Rilke's interest in the contemporary development of Freudian psychology. In its treatment of the child, the mother, the young man and the girl who is in love with him, this Elegy is an extraordinary mixture of bitterness and tenderness.

## Fourth Elegy

Again, lovers, interior landscape, child and parent, this time the father. And new images—theatrical entertainment, with the puppet preferred to the dancer. The boy with the squint is Rilke's cousin Egon, who died young and is commemorated in the *Sonnets to Orpheus*, II, 8. The German word for puppet, *puppe*, also means doll, making the transition to the child among his playthings even more natural. The image of the child will remind some readers of Wordsworth, but Wordsworth's has intimations of immortality, while Rilke's is closer to an understanding and acceptance of death.

## Fifth Elegy

In the summer of 1915 Rilke stayed in Frau Hertha von Koenig's Munich apartment, where Picasso's painting of a performing troup, *Les Saltimbanques*, hung (it is now in the National Gallery in Washington). This Elegy is partly inspired by that painting. Rilke seems to have noticed that the group of clowns forms a D shape, and he takes that to stand for *Dastehn*, "thereness," or "standing-thereness," with overtones of *Dasein*, "existence." The problem of making the D the capital letter of a word in English ("Duration"?) is the sort of thing that makes translators despair.

*Augustus the Strong:* Elector of Saxony, 1670–1733, who practiced feats of strength to entertain his guests, here bending a pewter plate with one hand.

*the rose of watching . . .:* a good example of Rilke's imagery at its most complex. The knot of spectators around the acrobats resembles a flower, gaining or losing petals as watchers arrive and leave. Its center, where the performers bounce and tumble, is both a pestel and the flower's pistil whose pollen (perhaps the dust they stir up) goes nowhere, but refertilizes its own blossom, leading to a false fruition. This is one of many images comparing and contrasting human life to flowers, trees, fruit, and pollination.

*Subrisio Saltat.:* an abbreviation of *subrisio saltatoris*, acrobat's smile.

*Angel: suppose there's a place:* like the Fourth Elegy, the Fifth begins with a vision of unsatisfactory art (in both cases, performance) and closes with a vision in which the difficulties are resolved in the presence of death and a satisfactory performance is envisioned.

## *Sixth Elegy*

To the possible forms of idealized humanity—those who died young, lovers, children, performing artists—whose attempts to fulfill the ideal cause various forms of anguish, Rilke now adds the hero. It is as if the epic hero has suddenly come into the poem, almost as an afterthought. It is a wonderfully subtle portrait, focusing as it does not so much on the hero as on analogies (e.g. the fig tree) and effects (on children, mothers, lovers, and "each heart"). There is something faintly comic about the hero's first asserting himself as a sperm cell. Heroes may be wonderful, but the role is reserved for the few and is as distant, somehow, as a legend.

*Karnak:* ancient Egyptian holy place, site of many temples and ruins. Rilke had visited it in 1911. The image here seems to be that characteristic depiction of the conqueror, smiling in his chariot as he is pulled by horses who smile the same smile. The smile is another recurrent image in the *Elegies.*

## *Seventh Elegy*

The poem now turns from life-transcendence, as envisioned in the ideal performances and the hero, to life-acceptance. The wooing voice, motivated by desire for a less transient state of being, is rejected, and the poem performs a kind of backward somersault into a beautiful image of a summer dawn. Now the dead seem to long for and seek out our earthly existence. And we are the ones who learn how to love and celebrate the visible, "to transform it within." Human imaginative achievement, as represented by music, architecture, and love, can now be understood and praised.

In the letter to his Polish translator (cited in the Introduction) Rilke wrote:

> Nature, the things we move among and use, are provisional and perishable; but, so long as we are here, they are *our* possession and our friendship, sharing the knowledge of our grief and gladness, as they have already been the confidants of our forebears. Hence it is important not only not to run down and degrade everything earthly, but just because of its temporariness, which it shares with us, we ought to grasp and transform these phenomena and these things in a most loving understanding. Transform? Yes; for our task is so deeply and so passionately to impress upon ourselves this provisional and perishable earth, that its essential being will arise again 'invisibly' in us. *We are the bees of the invisible. We frantically plunder the visible of its honey, to accumulate it in the great golden hive of the invisible.*

# Eighth Elegy

The celebration of human transience in the preceding Elegy is here sharply qualified. Self-consciousness, time-consciousness, and death-consciousness, which mark us off from animals and, at times, children and lovers, are Rilke's version of a fallen condition. As he pursues the idea he discovers that even animals may not be altogether at home in this existence because they may have some awareness of the contrast between the comfort of the womb and the exposure of birth. Only creatures like gnats, who come into being in the open air, can be completely at home in the world, taking it for a womb, a mother. If there is a humorous touch in the image of the gnat hopping happily on its wedding day, there is nothing of the kind in the poem's somber and splendid conclusion, one of those summaries of our life that give this poem its impressive scope. This Elegy is dedicated to Rudolf Kassner, an Austrian writer and thinker, because of discussions he and Rilke had at Duino about the preferability of certain states of existence (they did not agree) and such questions as the "happiness of the gnat."

## Ninth Elegy

The poem now swings back to something more like the mood of the Seventh Elegy. But praise and pain are tightly woven together by this point in the *Elegies*. We would choose human existence, the opening lines affirm, if we had the alternative of metamorphosis (like Daphne, evading love to become a laurel), but the justification of our choice would not be easy to explain. It becomes clear as the poem moves forward that given our limitation we must accept and celebrate not only our own perishability but that of the things around us. If music, architecture, sculpture, heroism, and love stood for the achievements of the human imagination before, poetry now begins to come into its own as Rilke considers the function of language itself as a means of identification and praise. The letter (quoted in the note, the *Seventh Elegy*) in which Rilke speaks of "the things we move among and use" as "*our* possession and our friendship," is relevant here as well.

## Tenth Elegy

Rilke takes several risks in this final Elegy. If the Third Elegy paralleled the epic descent to the underworld, this one seems to take us beyond life and into death in a way that no other poet has attempted. The narrative line and allegorical manner make this Elegy somewhat more accessible, but there is no slackening of imaginative intensity. After an opening 'prayer' of great beauty, we get the wry portrait of "Pain City," and then, in a kind of pastoral 'straying' into strange countryside, we cross that land— based partly on ancient Egypt, the most death-oriented civilization we have had—where visible and invisible are so astonishingly mingled. Motifs from the rest of the poem stream together in this Elegy, as in the list of constellations. And Rilke stretches our imaginative capabilities to their limits, as when we are asked to comprehend that the owl, startled from behind the edge of the Sphinx's crown, traces the shape of the huge face with one wing as it flies across and down it, a tracing which is transferred to the dead man's sharpened sense of hearing as if a book which already lay open could somehow be opened again! The ending of the poem either needs no explanation or simply lies beyond it.